PIANO | VOCAL | GUITAR

THE HUNGER GAMES
SONGS FROM DISTRICT 12 AND BEYOND

ISBN 978-1-4584-9117-6

HAL•LEONARD® CORPORATION

7777 W. BLUEMOUND RD. P.O. BOX 13819 MILWAUKEE, WI 53213

Visit Hal Leonard Online at
www.halleonard.com

CONTENTS

ABRAHAM'S DAUGHTER

Written by WIN BUTLER,
RÉGINE CHASSAGNE and T BONE BURNETT

TOMORROW WILL BE KINDER

Words and Music by LYDIA ROGERS
and LAURA ROGERS

NOTHING TO REMEMBER

Words and Music by
NEKO CASE

Slowly, Freely

You ___ told me some-thing that scared me to death.

Don't take me home; I can't face that yet. I'm a-shamed that I'm ___ bare-ly hu -

SAFE & SOUND

Words and Music by TAYLOR SWIFT,
T-BONE BURNETT, JOHN PAUL WHITE
and JOY WILLIAMS

Moderate Ballad

THE RULER AND THE KILLER

Words and Music by T BONE BURNETT,
SCOTT MESCUDI and GREG WELLS

Moderately slow

When I talk, you should lis - ten. _____
mind on the mis - sion. _____

DARK DAYS

Words and Music by
PUNCH BROTHERS

Slow half-time feel

Moth - er, lis - ten to my heart.

Moth - er, lis - ten to my heart.

Just as one beat ends, an - oth - er

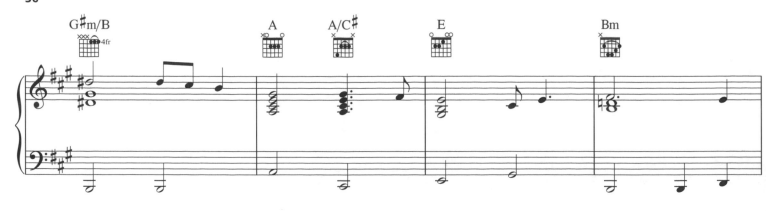

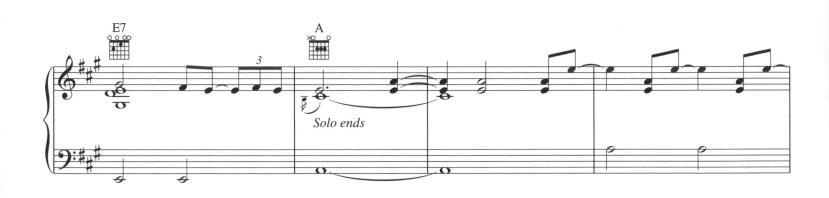

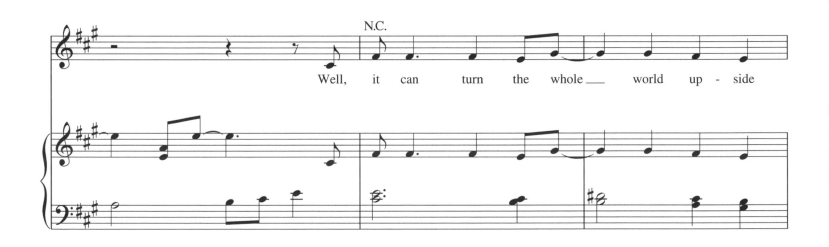

Well, it can turn the whole __ world up - side

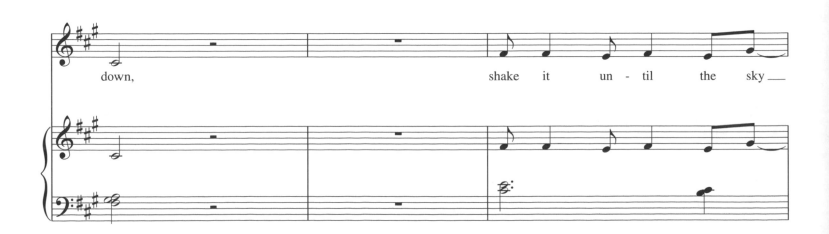

down, shake it un - til the sky __

just as one beat ends, an-
oth - er starts. You can hear no
(Mm.)
mat - ter where you are.

ONE ENGINE

Words and Music by
COLIN MELOY

Moderately fast

One en - gine
I'd like to

bare - ly makes it a - way.
get you in some kind of way.

* Recorded a half step lower.

DAUGHTER'S LAMENT

Words and Music by
RHIANNON GIDDENS

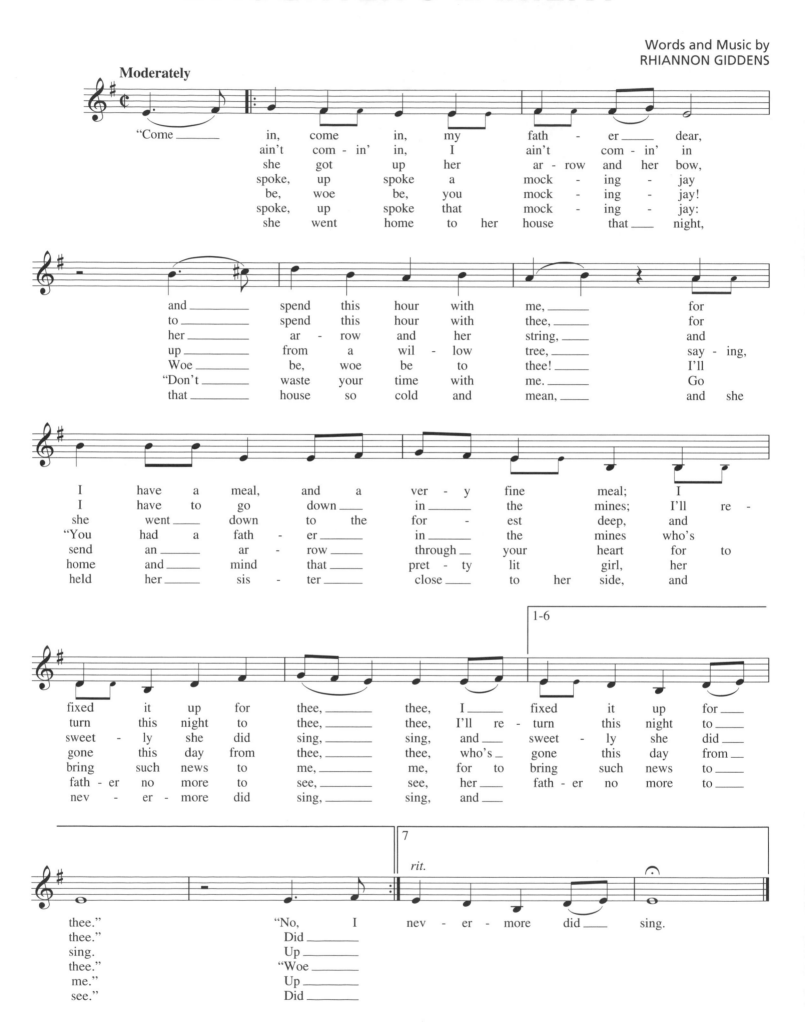

KINGDOM COME

Words and Music by JOHN PAUL WHITE
and JOY WILLIAMS

TAKE THE HEARTLAND

Words and Music by
GLEN HANSARD

You say sit, _____ you say stand, _ you say stop, ___ you say go, _ you say sit,

Take the heart - land.

Take the heart - land, your sense of re - venge. _

Take the heart - land, you make it look eas -

COME AWAY TO THE WATER

Words and Music by
GLEN HANSARD

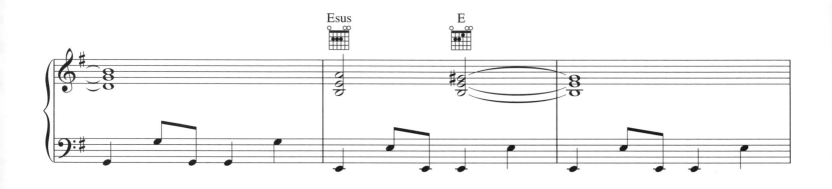

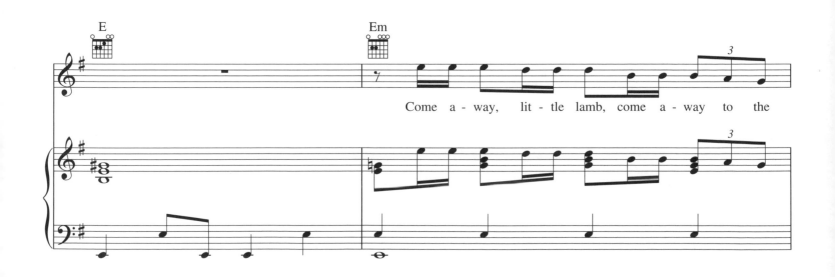

Come a - way, lit - tle lamb, come a - way to the

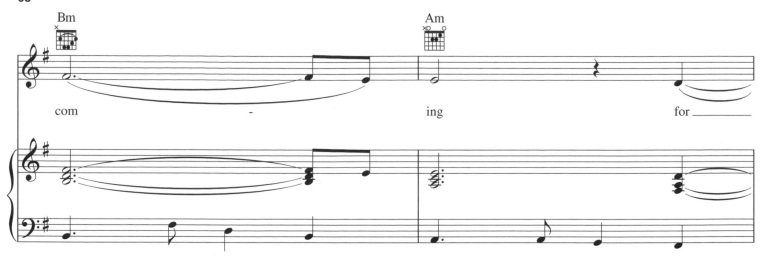

Bm   Am

com -   ing   for

Em

     you.

Play 3 times

RUN DADDY RUN

Words and Music by MIRANDA LAMBERT,
ASHLEY MONROE and ANGALEENA PRESLEY

Moderately

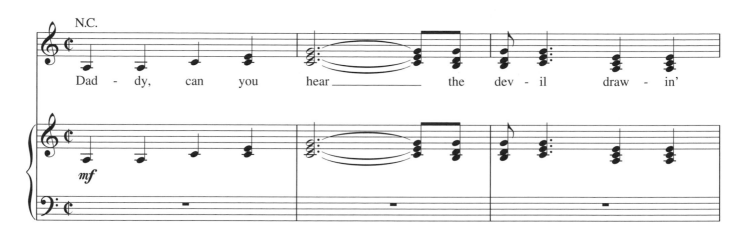

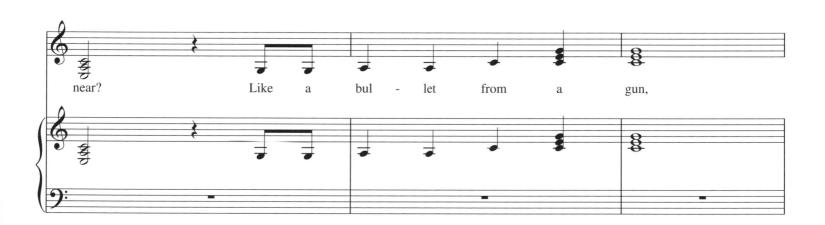

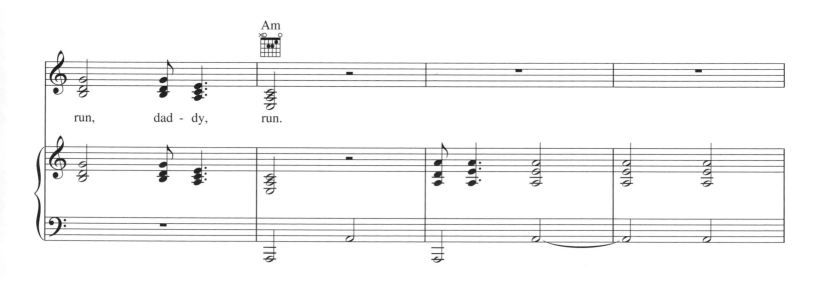

RULES

Written by MEGAN KEELY
and BRANDON KEELY

This blood keeps me a - live, _____ but
wa - ter in your eyes, _____ and I know

what is it _____ that runs _____ through you? _____
I'm _____ the rea - son that _____ it's there. _____

E - lec - tri - ci - ty _____ and wires _____ dic -
But still, I don't _____ feel bad, be - cause I

tat - ing ev - 'ry - thing _____ you do. _____
know that you have more _____ to spare. _____

Em7

You tell me that___ you hear___ me and
And just be-hind___ your eyes _____ are

Gmaj7/B

all your mem - o - ries are _____ real,
switch - es that can turn back _____ on

Em7

but how do I _____ know___ you don't just
to clear a - way___ to - day _____ 'til

Gmaj7/B

feel what you've been told to feel. ___
all your mem - o - ries are gone. ___

EYES OPEN

Words and Music by
TAYLOR SWIFT

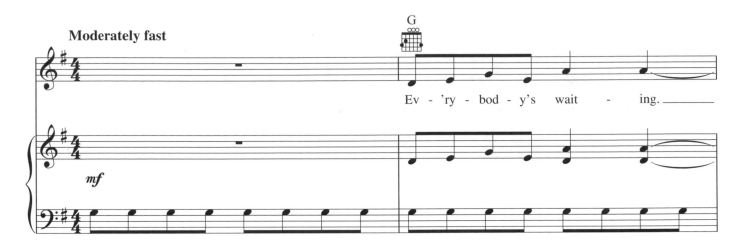

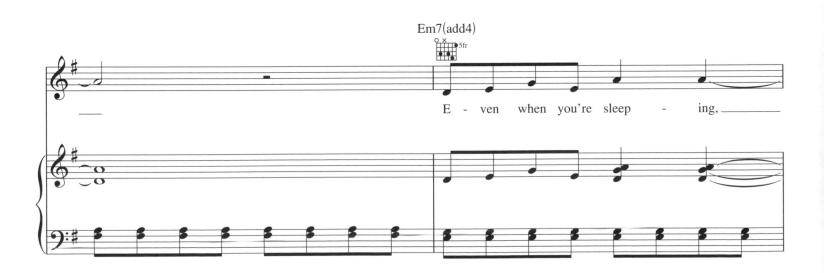

keep your eye eyes _____ o - pen.

LOVER IS CHILDLIKE

Words and Music by BEN KNOX MILLER,
JEFF PRYSTOWSKY and JOCELYN ADAMS

at Co - ney Is - land;

we'll go out _____ on the sea. _____

So don't ask _____ me no ques - tions, _____
See the fish _____ swim - ming up - stream, _

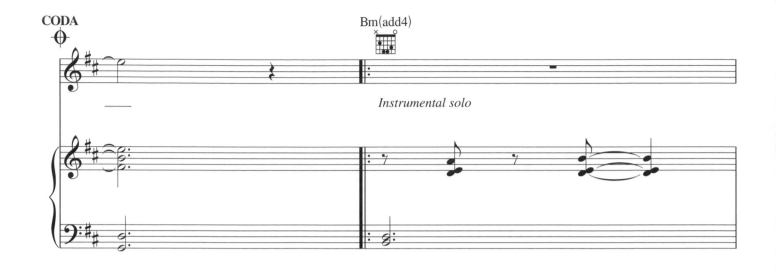

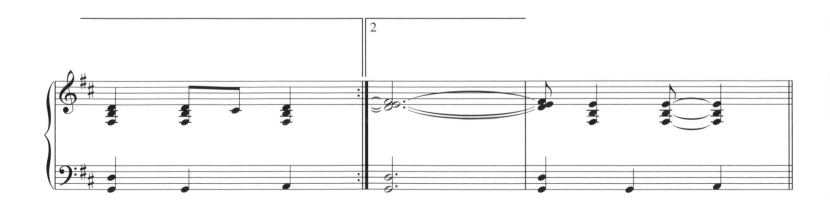

While the band ___ plays the an - them,

she whis - pers, _____ "God hates ___ flags." ___

Repeat and Fade

Optional Ending

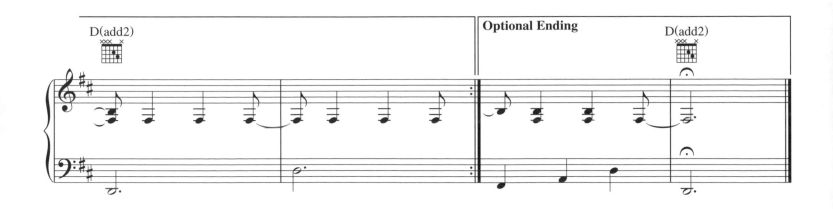

JUST A GAME

Words and Music by
JASMINE VAN DEN BOGAERDE